A Guide For Customer Service In The Beauty Industry

To order additional copies, please contact us.
BookSurge, LLC
www.booksurge.com
1-866-308-6235
orders@booksurge.com

A Guide for Customer Service in the Beauty Industry

Troi Martin

2005

A Guide For Customer Service In The Beauty Industry

CONTENTS

CERTAIN QUALIFICATIONS ONE MUST HAVE TO SERVICE THE BEAUTY INDUSTRY

1. You must work well with other people and strive to be friends with fellow staff members and clients.

2. Superior customer service is a challenge you should welcome each and every day.

3. Your daily mission should be to treat your clients as loving family members.

4. You should continuously search for information to educate yourself on new treatments, products and procedures to share with clients.

5. Educate and prepare yourself to answer questions as accurately as possible in order to inform clients about the industry.

6. You should crave customer contact and interactions with clients as well as fellow staff members.

7. Perform well in fragile and pressure situations.

8. Enjoy entertaining customers and clients.

9. Be strong enough to be a leader and secure enough to follow

10. Be organized. Your work place is a reflection of your professional skills

11. Respect and value other people's time.

12. Be energetic and enthusiastic.

13. Respect individuality.

14. Remember your personal appearance is a reflection of your professionalism.

15. Try to make people smile.

16. Provide a soothing and calm atmosphere for your clients

17. Protect your clients' and patients' privacy.

18. Understand that providing a good first impression is the most cost effective way to assure repeat buisness from happy patients/clients.

ACTION PLAN WORK SHEET

_____

_____

_____

_____

_____

_____

_____

_____

_____

_____

_____

_____

_____

_____

_____

_____

_____

_____

_____

THE TEN COMMANDMENTS OF THE BEAUTY INDUSTRY

I.   Quality of work is more important than quantity.

2.   Treat your clients like loving relatives.

3.   Always protect your clients - emotionally, physically and confidentially.

4.   Never let a client or patient walk out the door in poor condition.

5.   Always do your best to understand the client's expectations.

6.   Experiment without risks.

7.   Appearance is second to integrity.

8.   Change is growth.

9. The first thing we create is trust.

10. Thou shall not criticize one's neighbor

ACTION PLAN WORK SHEET

_____

_____

_____

_____

_____

_____

_____

_____

_____

_____

_____

_____

_____

_____

_____

_____

_____

_____

_____

DEFINING YOUR MISSION

ASK YOURSELF AND OTHERS THESE QUESTIONS DUR-ING STAFF MEETINGS:

** Why do customers and patients remember me?

** How do customers feel about me after they have received my services?

** What do customers tell their friends and relatives about my services?

** In what ways do I assist my fellow team members?

** In regards to the customer, what is the major purpose of my services?

** Have I been supportive of my doctor, manager and/or boss in building our business?

** What do I do if I cannot fulfill our clients' requests?

** Do I return calls and complete work when I said I would?

** Have I perfected my telephone personality?

** Have I perfected my listening skills?

** Do my patients and clients enjoy me?

ACTION PLAN WORK SHEET

_____

_____

_____

_____

_____

_____

_____

_____

_____

_____

_____

_____

_____

_____

_____

_____

_____

"MAY I HELP YOU?" WISDOM

- When a customer asks you a question, the answer becomes your responsibility.

- RELATIONSHIP - (Latin: referre) the state of being mutually interested. Reverence or respect for another. To be involved.

- Perceptions are your choice—at the end of the day, ask yourself how you rate with your clients, on a scale from one to ten.

- ORGANIZED - (Greek: organon) Prepared for future situations.

- Customer service has three parts: mental, emotional and physical. It is like a three-legged stool; which leg is more important?

- When a customer walks out of your place of business with a smile on their face—*that* is a marketable product.

- Self respect will always triumph over disrespect.

- ATTITUDE - (Latin: aptus) State of mind.

- We never plan to fail serving our customers but we often fail to plan.

- ENTHUSIASM - (Greek: enter+theos) Desire to achieve; excited about learning.

- One of the best stress reducers is to see a smile on a customer's face.

- People solve problems; technology only helps to make the solutions faster.

- The best service in the world is not necessarily flawless, but it is always sincere.

- A sense of humor is the most powerful weapon against frustration.

- MOTIVATION—(Latin: movere) something within the individual, rather than outside, which incites him or her to action.

- The relationship you have with your customer starts with the one you have with yourself.

ACTION PLAN WORK SHEET

_____

_____

_____

_____

_____

_____

_____

_____

_____

_____

_____

_____

_____

_____

_____

_____

_____

_____

_____

WHEN? WHERE? WHY? WHAT? WHO?

OUTSTANDING CUSTOMER SERVICE

The time for training to become an outstanding customer service person should have started well before we ever entered kindergarten. According to many top customer service professionals, the current generation getting ready to enter the job market has lower than accepted standards, and lacks the basic ingredients for customer service careers. With that in mind, invest in educating yourself through seminars, hands-on work shops, training manuals and by observing other customer service personnel who are on their way to becoming the most out standing staff members in your business.

KNOWLEDGE ALWAYS PAYS OFF

The Beauty Industry is all about customer service and product satisfaction. If you work for a doctor, a salon, or a day spa you're proud of, then by all means let everyone know it. Show off your business and inform your customers why your business is the best at what it does. If you're not proud of your business situation, think about changing jobs or even careers. Trying to motivate yourself in a job you don't appreciate is nearly impossible. You can only truly benefit psychologically if you are proud of your business.

A very important trait to learn, when dealing with patients, clients, or customers, is to know how to LISTEN SINCERELY to your clients. Other than the actual outcome of your client's treatments and procedures, SINCERE LISTENING is one of the most important things you can do for them.

Begin everyday by preparing yourself to improve your business financially and personally. Keep notes and records so you may remember where you left off so your growth can be measured each day.

Equip yourself and your fellow customer service representatives with information, tools, techniques and ideas that will assist in creating positive customer transactions. Continue to grow by SHARING ideas on how to better your business environment.

A newspaper advertisement may start the flame of interest. However, reinforcing great service experiences fuels the loyal customer. Interaction with beauty clients can be very fragile, unlike other service-oriented positions like plumbers, gardeners, painters, etc. The beauty clients and patients today demand full attention given to their needs. This must CONTINUE throughout their relationship with your business, or they will seek out for a different customer service relationship that they may bond with.

In today's cosmetic and plastic surgery offices and salons, most staff members have some form of training about the services and procedures their business provides.

To becoming outstanding in the customer service department you must know how to best *present* these services. This takes an entirely different talent. Timing is very important in delivering information to potential clients. When to say what, and how to say it, can make or break a client's decision on where she/he will choose to have their beauty services completed. Take your time in explaining questions asked by clients, don't rush your answers, and if you need to call the customer back, do so. Always make sure their questions are *completely* answered. Make sure that they know your name and/or who to call if they have any questions and/or concerns.

> "You just can't over do
> superior customer service."
>
> — Troi Martin

WHERE

MEDICAL OFFICES, SPAS and SALONS

Patients, clients and customers are very aware of their surroundings when seeking elective services. Studies indicate that customers of cosmetic services expect both exceptional service as well as a professional, pleasant atmosphere. Staff members need to pay very close attention to what their clients' reactions are to the business atmosphere. If a patient or client is uncomfortable with his or her surroundings, there is a good chance that they will be uncomfortable with their service and less likely that they return as a happy customer.

Staff members must be taught the skills they'll need to address patients and clients about having the right attitude. However, the place of service must also have the right attitude. The decor and even the smell affect the consumer's decisions. "Clean", "warm" and "professional" are the three main words they'll use to describe your business to their friends and relatives.

The secret to standing out in the beauty industry is to EXCEED THE CUSTOMER'S EXPECTATIONS. A beautiful office with a snack bar is wonderful, but taking orders for what the patient would like to have in her new home away from home is exceptional. For example, keep a suggestion form next to your refreshment bar. This will give the patient a chance to start an interaction with your business.

WHY

ELECTIVE SERVICES

You must ask yourself, is this career for me?

Then ask yourself why clients choose elective procedures which they obviously could live without. You'll find that the answer is usually the same: the procedures make them/us feel good.

Arm yourself with knowledge about the elective services available - medical, cosmetic, etc. If it involves personal appearance of any kind, consider it part of your field. This knowledge will help you to understand what the best possible option is for your clients. Knowledge of these services will also help you to make the right recommendation. You will become a loyal source for your customers. They will rely on you, and will share their experiences with friends and relatives.

For example, if you are a hairdresser, and you have clients who are losing their hair, you feel that a hair transplant may be of interest to them. First of all, make sure that you are informed about the procedure and then share your opinion with them. Make an appointment with a Cosmetic Surgeon, and educate yourself regarding the latest techniques. Or if you work in a Plastic Surgeon's office and you have clients who want thicker looking lashes, educate yourself about permanent cosmetics. Have a permanent cosmetic tech come to your office and explain what she has to offer. Share and search out all the information that is available to arm yourself with the power of beauty knowledge. With all the procedures and treatments available today, it is up to you to explain to your clients how wonderful the beauty industry can be and how you can help them to enhance their lives. The best way to protect your self from unhappy clients is to help them understand unrealistic expectations. Spend as much time as is needed to explain what a procedure can and cannot do for them.

SUPERIOR CUSTOMER SERVICE MEANS:

*Doing ordinary things extraordinarily well. *Going beyond what's expected.

*Adding value and integrity to every customer. *Discovering new ways to delight your client.

*Taking care of your customers as you would take care of your grandmother.

WHAT

THE BEAUTY INDUSTRY

The industry of looks and beauty has been around since the day the mirror was invented and will always be a driving force in our society. It's a well-known fact that if we feel we look good, we generally feel pretty good about ourselves. Physical appearance, inherited or acquired, affects self image and interaction with others.

Cosmetic and plastic surgeons, hairdressers, skin professionals Image consultants, are called upon daily to help the public look and feel better. These professional have many common benefits to share, but there is one thing that stands out in the beauty industry from all other professions: We truly can help people feel good!

Giving a client the right haircut, make-up and/or wardrobe can literally change a person's outlook on life, and in return, life's outlook on them. Patients who venture into the cosmetic surgery world have found themselves to feel more confident and look forward to sharing their experiences with others.

> **"Even though one doesn't need**
> **a prescription for a hair cut, a new**
> **outfit, or an eye lift, these look-good,**
> **Feel-good treatments can be the best**
> **anti-depressant money can buy."**

> **- Troi Martin**

In the beauty world you might be excused once by a devoted customer, but a first time customer may be turned off permanently by a single experience that contradicts the expectations of a superior customer service business. The customer who seeks out professional beauty consultants for advice has pre-set high expectations for their anticipated service.

As stated before in this guide, *generic* customer service is not good enough in the beauty industry. Clients, patients, and customers will not return for services with your business, if you do not deliver superior customer service.

LOYAL CLIENTS ARE GAINED BY BEHAVIOR THAT GROWS OUT OF CONSISTENT EXPERIENCES.

WHO

BUILDING RELATIONSHIPS
WITH CLIENTS

Practicing with integrity must always mean "doing what is best for your customers". Today's consumers are very smart and picky about their choices for elective services - show them that there is no need to go elsewhere. The work of your educated team will guarantee your clients, patients and customers, treatment provided with superior customer service.

Respect your customer's *time*—and you will earn their respect in return. Always make sure that you are sincerely concerned about your clients. Often times, some may have to wait their turn, however, always make yourself available. Building a solid, long term relationship with anyone is time consuming. So invest plenty of time to get to know your customers. They will be loyal clients once you have convinced them that you are very dedicated in servicing their needs.

A nice chair and pleasant waiting room can help a customer feel comfortable, but a pat on the back, or an inviting look from you and your staff members can help make the customer feel secure about having chosen your business. Every customer deserves your attention. Acknowledging someone is giving them respectful time. Customers, clients and patients yearn for your undivided attention and time.

The term "quality of care" is so widely used in customer service and falls way short of what is needed for the Beauty Industry business in order to deliver what is considered, superior customer service. We must always represent our doctor's office and salons even when we are not at our business location. Appearance and respectful manor outside of work should always be taken into consideration. Become a part of your business and allow your business to become a part of you. Your customers will associate you with your place of employment, whenever and wherever they meet you.

So, take pride in that. Make your clients proud that you are the business of their choice.

Your patients and clients are there for you to help them—not the other way around. Leave your problems and bad moods at home. Remind yourself daily that part of your work is to present to your customers the best possible outlook on life, and deliver outstanding service. Help your co-workers get through tough times and keep the uplifting outlook your offices and salons need to project.

Motivating others can be very stimulating by itself. Customers, co-workers and bosses will all recognize and remember the person who can and will put a smile on their face.

Ask your customers many questions. "Would you like something to drink?" "Can I help you with your gown?" "Do you need anything?" "What else can we do for you today?" are just examples.

Questions and your genuine concern are the most endearing action your customers will remember. Questions about information, although very important, are common and will most likely be forgotten. However, questions of concern will be remembered and they help to form a bond between yourself and your customer.

The happiest workers are those who have invested their time and energy in delivering superior customer service. Investing in your work must start at bonding with your customers, clients, and patients.

Although still important, "smile training" is not good enough anymore. Staff members in the Beauty Industry must go much further with extending their welcoming to clients; addressing them in a sincere and dedicated way is a must today. Make sure that you have always made good eye contact with your client, and if possible, make contact in the form of a handshake, a touch on the arm or a small hug.

Start every day as though you are meeting new family members, this can be a helpful way of programming yourself into a consistently cheery state of mind. Always remember that bonding with a client is assuring her/him to return for services. If no bonding takes place during their visit to your office, spa, or salon, these customers will most likely seek out other businesses until a connection and a bond have been formed.

For every customer lost, companies must spend six times more revenue on acquiring a replacement that it would have cost them to incorporate customer loyalty strategies into their customer service efforts.

- Harvard Business Review

ACTION PLAN WORK SHEET

_____

_____

_____

_____

_____

_____

_____

_____

_____

_____

_____

_____

_____

_____

_____

_____

_____

APPEARANCE

What is an Image Consultant?

An Image Consultant is a person who specializes in visual appearance, as well as verbal and non-verbal communication. An Image Consultant counsels individuals and corporate clients on appearance, behavior and communication skills.

The Beauty Industry has many different areas of expertise: hair, skin, teeth and nail, professionals, Cosmetic and Plastic Surgeons, Cosmetic Dentists and Image Consultants etc. All play a part in helping clients, patients and customers achieve their desired style and look.

Generic customer service isn't good enough anymore in the Beauty Industry. And all who have elected to venture into this field of appearance must be impeccable with their own look. If your position requires you to wear a uniform or medical scrubs, it is not acceptable for your hair, skin and nails to not be done up. Hairdressers and make-up artist must be fashionable and in the trend in order to advance in the Beauty Industry, or clients will move on to a more impressionable stylist.

People who are working in the Beauty Industry have become role models in the public's eyes. Cosmetic Surgeons, Cosmetic Dentists, Hair-dressers, Image Consultants etc. are landing their own television shows, and are becoming more popular than traditional entertainment. The craving for information about style, fashion and cosmetic surgery has become one of the most popular subjects for today's female consumer.

As a beauty advisor, make your first impression your best impression, through professional looking clothes, skin and hair styles. You can't just act like a leader, you must look like one, in order for your customers to believe in you and pay for your services.

I think we can all agree how disappointing it is to see a beautiful movie star caught by the press and looking ragged. Customers and clients feel the same way when they see members of the beauty staff not concerned with their appearance.

Image matters a great deal to most companies, yet can be a highly personal and sensitive issue when communicating expectations to staff members.

However, in the Beauty Industry, there's quite simply, no room for a sloppy, unkept person. The bottom line is straight forward: Change careers if looking professional and being fashionable are a problem.

What you wear and how you look tells customers more about your business than many realize. The style of your clothes and how much attention you pay to details will inform your customers how much you care about your job position.

Does it really matter?
What a bride and groom wear on their wedding day?
What a policeman wears while he is on duty?
What a judge wears in the courtroom?
What a surgeon wears when performing surgery?

And the answer is, of course, absolutely.

"Your appearance will affect the way your customers perceive your service."

Troi Martin

ACTION PLAN WORK SHEET

_____

_____

_____

_____

_____

_____

_____

_____

_____

_____

_____

_____

_____

_____

_____

_____

_____

SURVEY SAYS

(530) Patients, Customers and Clients surveyed

COMMENTS ABOUT STAFF

#3 - Appearance (skin, hair, nails, clothing etc)
#2 - Attention given to customers
#1 - *Polite or rude office staff*

COMMENTS ABOUT OFFICE AND SALON

#4 - Smell (odor of office)
#3 - Location (easy or hard to find)
#2 - Décor (warm, professional, clean, etc.)
#1 - *Does the office or salon run on time*

WHAT PATIENTS WANT TO KNOW MOST ABOUT THEIR COSMETIC SURGEON

#6 - What surgeries has the doctor had done?

#5 - Has the doctor performed surgeries on any celebrities?

#4 - What surgeries has his wife had done?

#3 - How old is the doctor?

#2 - Is the doctor married?

#1 - *How long has the doctor been performing Surgery?*

ACTION PLAN WORK SHEET

_____

_____

_____

_____

_____

_____

_____

_____

_____

_____

_____

_____

_____

_____

_____

_____

_____

_____

_____

THAT'S JUST RUDE!

To get a clear understanding of the term RUDE, let's look at its definition:

RUDE-(Latin, Greek, any language) - Lacking the graces and refinement of polished and skilled characteristics; disrespectful

One person's "rude" might be another person's "habit." The fact is, the offended party is the real judge of whether something is rude or not (unless your boss says otherwise).

To make rudeness easier to identify, let's examine the many different types of rude actions.

Type I:
Accidental Rudeness by Omission.
This is inadvertent rudeness caused by lack of action.
Examples:

A.   Forgetting to RSVP to a function/meeting
B.   Being so focused that you ignore others around you

Type 2:
Accidental Rudeness by Commission which is inadvertent rudeness caused by something you did.

Examples:

A.   Inappropriate, or lack of, manners
B.   Ignoring a client's presence

Type 3:
Intentional Rudeness by Omission,
Purposeful rudeness caused by lack of action. Examples:

A.   Not returning voice messages/emails or phone calls, business or personal
B.   Leaving a mess with the intention of having others clean it up

Type 4:
Intentional Rudeness by Commission.
This is rudeness delivered on purpose and caused by an action you took. This is industrial strength rudeness with the intention of sending a message.

A.   Intentionally being nasty, hurtful and/or sarcastic
B.   One-word answers, cold replies, having an "attack tone" to statements

Rude is a crucial topic in customer service. One rude day can destroy years of genuine sincere customer rapport with a client or patient. For any business, politeness is important but it is imperative in the elective services business.

Beauty Industry means one word: **special**

"Show me a polite receptionist, nurse, doctor or hairdresser and I will show you a successful business person."

- Troi Martin

ACTION PLAN WORK SHEET

_____

_____

_____

_____

_____

_____

_____

_____

_____

_____

_____

_____

_____

_____

_____

_____

_____

_____

_____

_____

_____

SERVICE READY

Here are some questions to help "Service Ready" your practice and or business.

1. When handling calls from your customers, are all of your team members employing an effective, uniform greeting?

2. Has your entire staff been comprehensively trained on the techniques needed to handle, defuse and retain angry customers/patients?

3. Are your staff members trained in the delicate area of delivering negative information in a positive way (when needed)?

4. Is your staff equipped with the skills of knowing how and when to use a variety of questioning techniques in their customer interaction, in order to sell your services with the most advantage?

5. When a team member has a performance shortfall, are your managers trained to implement a proven coaching process?

6. Does your staff have the tools to build a strong, positive rapport with your customers and patients?

7. When a team member is having a bad day, does your business have a plan to never let the customers see any negative emotions?

8. When immediate action is necessary to make a service recovery, are your team members trained for a quick mending?

"If you are not prepared to be service ready, you will always be in service recovery. Service recovery is not just fixing the problem. It's making sure it won't happen again"

- Troi Martin

ACTION PLAN WORK SHEET

_____

_____

_____

_____

_____

_____

_____

_____

_____

_____

_____

_____

_____

_____

_____

_____

_____

_____

HUMOR HELPS

Have each staff member take turns posting monthly "HUMOR HELPS" throughout your office. Have copies available for customers to take home - printed on your office stationary.

EXAMPLES:

Getting older is beyond our control. No matter how much we'd like to, we can't stop time from marching on. However, growing old is something we can control. That's where attitude enters in.

When we look in the mirror, we can either count our wrinkles or count our blessings that we have the best trained Beauty Professionals in the world available that we can count on!

The young are happy because they have the ability to see beauty. Anyone who keeps the ability to see beauty never grows old.

The minute you settle for less than you deserve, you get less than you settled for.

Life is a great big canvas, and you should throw all the paint and mascara on it you can.

I love long walks, especially when taken by people who annoy me.

Customer/Patient Evaluation

GIVE TO CUSTOMER AFTER SHE HAS COMPLETED HER TREATMENTS

Name_____

Attitude_____

On Time
Always__Never__Only when hungry__

Treatment results
Average__Above Average__Can now milk a cow_

Weight Control
__Eats like a Bird
__Hotty
__Eats too many Birds

We here at *your business name*
__ Enjoy your visits with us
__ Need to take sedatives before you arrive
__ Need to take sedatives after you leave

When scheduling your appointments
__Please inform the receptionist you are a
  V.I.P customer
__Please inform the front desk if you need help
  with parking your broom stick
__Please inform the receptionist your check still
  can bounce like a Kangaroo

ACTION PLAN WORK SHEET

_____

_____

_____

_____

_____

_____

_____

_____

_____

_____

_____

_____

_____

_____

_____

_____

_____

_____

_____

"BAY" PRODUCTIONZ
YOUR ONE STOP SHOP FOR PRESENTATIONS

WWW.BAYPRODUCTIONZ.COM

MARKETING YOUR SUPERIOR

CUSTOMER SERVICE

To succeed in the Beauty Industry, your business must attract and retain a growing base of satisfied customers.

The average customer/patient seeking services from Beauty Consultants will, most likely, not be purchasing on impulse. A strategic plan and a process of elimination of different businesses, is usually how a potential customer decides when and where to make an appointment for your services.

SEMINARS

Conducting seminars provides a great opportunity to advertise your company's name in newspapers, flyers, on your website, or any place where potential customers may see your advertisement. A professionally prepared PowerPoint presentation is a most effective tool in delivering your information to potential customers.

POWERPOINT PRESENTATIONS

Whether your services are provided in a Doctor's office, hair salon or as an Image Consultant, you must utilize the latest technology in sharing your information with consumers. Merely mailing out a brochure with your information on it is becoming rapidly outdated in today's Beauty Industry.

Market your business the new tech way and have a custom Power-Point Presentation about your office or salon designed with information about you and your business.

ACTION PLAN WORK SHEET

_____

_____

_____

_____

_____

_____

_____

_____

_____

_____

_____

_____

_____

_____

_____

_____

_____

_____

_____